Unlocking the Mind:

The Power of Neuro-Linguistic Programming in Cognitive Behavioural Therapy

By Rex Morton

Disclaimer

This book is intended to provide information about the fields of Neuro-Linguistic Programming (NLP) and Cognitive Behavioural Therapy (CBT) and their potential integration. While the author has made every effort to ensure that the information was correct at the time of publication, the author does not assume and hereby disclaims any liability to any party for any loss, damage, or disruption caused by errors or omissions, whether such errors or omissions result from negligence, accident, or any other cause.

The contents of this book should not be used as a substitute for professional advice, diagnosis, or treatment. The reader should always consult a qualified healthcare provider about mental health concerns or conditions. Never disregard professional psychological or medical advice or delay in seeking it because of something you have read in this book.

The views expressed in this work are solely those of the author and do not necessarily reflect the views of the publisher, and the publisher hereby disclaims any responsibility for them.

Including websites, links, or references to other resources does not mean that the author or the publisher endorses the information the organization or website may provide or its recommendations. Furthermore, the author does not guarantee the accuracy of these resources' information.

The use of any information provided in this book is solely at your own risk.

Introduction

The human mind, with its complexity and depth, has been a subject of fascination and inquiry for centuries. Over time, this curiosity has given birth to numerous approaches aimed at understanding and influencing human cognition and Behaviour. Among these approaches, Neuro-Linguistic Programming (NLP) and Cognitive Behavioural Therapy (CBT) have garnered significant attention for their distinct yet complementary strategies.

In the 1970s, Neuro-Linguistic Programming emerged as an innovative approach to communication, personal growth, and psychotherapy. Pioneered by Richard Bandler and John Grinder, NLP is premised on the idea that people's thoughts, feelings, and Behaviours are influenced by the intricate interplay between neurology, language, and patterns or 'programs' of Behaviour. The growing interest in NLP stems from its unique ability to provide practical techniques for self-improvement and transformative change.

On the other hand, Cognitive Behavioural Therapy, with its roots in the cognitive revolution of the 1960s, remains one of the most widely utilized therapeutic approaches today. The primary goal of CBT is to help individuals understand how their thoughts and perceptions can affect their feelings and Behaviours. This understanding then forms the basis for effective strategies to manage or overcome various psychological challenges.

Recently, there has been growing interest in integrating NLP techniques into various therapeutic approaches, including CBT. The aim of this book is to explore the effectiveness of this integration and highlight how NLP can enhance the outcomes of Cognitive Behavioural Therapy. This exploration will include a comprehensive overview of NLP and CBT, detailed discussions of their integration, practical examples of NLP techniques in CBT, and a review of empirical evidence s
upporting this approach.

Here is the chapter breakdown:

Chapter 1: Understanding Neuro-Linguistic Programming

Neuro-Linguistic Programming can be understood as a model and a set of tools designed to understand and influence human experience. This chapter will provide a comprehensive overview of NLP, including its history, principles, and core techniques. It will delve into the three key components of NLP: neurology, language, and programming, and explain how they interact to shape human Behaviour. The underlying assumptions of NLP and its connection to cognitive processes will also be illuminated.

Chapter 2: Foundations of Cognitive Behavioural Therapy

The second chapter will introduce the fundamental principles of Cognitive Behavioural Therapy and its evolution as a prominent therapeutic approach. It will discuss the theoretical underpinnings of CBT, including cognitive and Behavioural theories, and highlight the effectiveness of CBT in treating various psychological disorders.

Chapter 3: The Integration of NLP and CBT

Building on the understanding of both NLP and CBT, this chapter will examine the rationale behind combining these techniques. It will explore the shared elements between NLP and CBT, such as the focus on thoughts, emotions, and Behaviour. Case studies and research findings demonstrating the potential benefits of integrating NLP into CBT will also be presented.

Chapter 4: NLP Techniques in CBT

Chapter four will provide a detailed exploration of specific NLP techniques that can be integrated into CBT sessions. Techniques such as reframing, anchoring, and language patterns will be discussed, and their potential to enhance the effectiveness of

CBT interventions will be highlighted. Practical examples and step-by-step instructions will be included to facilitate understanding and implementation.

Chapter 5: Empirical Evidence and Research

A critical review of empirical studies and research conducted on the effectiveness of NLP techniques in CBT will be the focus of the fifth chapter. The limitations and strengths of existing research methodologies will be evaluated, and the implications of the findings and their significance for clinical practice will be discussed.

Chapter 6: Ethical Considerationsand Challenges

While the integration of NLP and CBT offers promising therapeutic possibilities, it also raises potential ethical concerns. This chapter will address these concerns and explore the challenges and limitations of using NLP techniques within a therapeutic context. It will offer guidelines for therapists to ensure the ethical and responsible application of these techniques.

The journey of exploring the effectiveness of NLP in CBT will culminate with a summary of the key findings and insights. The potential benefits and challenges of incorporating NLP techniques in clinical practice will be highlighted. Furthermore, the conclusion will discuss future directions for research and the continued exploration of NLP within the field of psychotherapy. It is hoped that this exploration will contribute to a broader understanding and appreciation of the transformative power of integrating Neuro-Linguistic Programming in Cognitive Behavioural Therapy.

Chapter 1: Understanding Neuro-Linguistic Programming

Neuro-Linguistic Programming (NLP) is often described as a toolkit for the mind, providing a model and practical techniques designed to understand and influence human experience. To truly comprehend the power and potential of NLP, we need to delve into its roots, core principles, and techniques.

History of Neuro-Linguistic Programming

NLP was conceived in the 1970s by Richard Bandler, a mathematician and information scientist, and John Grinder, a linguist. They were interested in understanding how people with extraordinary abilities achieved their successes. Their studies led them to create a model that aimed to replicate these patterns of success. This model became known as Neuro-Linguistic Programming, a term that encapsulates the core components of the approach: neurology, language, and programming.

**Key Components of NLP: Neurology, Language, and
Programming**

**The term 'Neuro-Linguistic Programming' is derived from three
essential elements:**

Neurology: The 'neuro' in NLP refers to the neurological system.
NLP recognizes that all Behaviour stems from our neurological
processes of sight, hearing, smell, taste, touch, and feeling. We
experience the world through our senses, and this experience is
processed through our nervous system.

Language: The 'linguistic' in Neuro-Linguistic Programming
refers to how we use language to make sense of our experiences
and to communicate those experiences. In this context,
language includes non-verbal communication such as body
language and facial expressions in addition to spoken or written
words.

Programming: The 'programming' component of NLP refers to
the patterns and sequences of thoughts and Behaviours we use
to achieve our goals. These patterns, or 'programs,' can be
modified or replaced with more effective ones using NLP
techniques.

These three components interact in complex ways to shape our experience of the world and our responses to it.

Core Principles and Techniques of NLP

There are several underlying assumptions or principles that guide the practice of NLP. These include:

The Map is Not the Territory: This principle suggests that our mental 'maps' or perceptions of the world do not fully represent the world itself. We all have unique perceptions based on our experiences, beliefs, values, and cultural backgrounds. NLP aims to help individuals recognize and challenge these maps when they are unhelpful or limiting.

You Cannot Not Communicate: This principle acknowledges that we communicate constantly, even when we believe we are not. Nonverbal cues, body language, and even silence convey messages that others can'read'.

The Meaning of Communication is the Response You Get: In NLP, the focus is on the effect of communication rather than the intended message. If a communication elicits an unexpected response, it's up to the communicator to change their approach.

There is No Failure, Only Feedback: This principle encourages a shift in perception where 'failures' are seen as opportunities for learning and growth.

Some of the core NLP techniques include anchoring, reframing, modeling, and the use of language patterns. These techniques are designed to help individuals change unhelpful thought patterns, beliefs, and Behaviours and replace them with more beneficial ones.

Connection to Cognitive Processes

NLP is deeply connected to cognitive processes. It recognizes that our thoughts, beliefs, and perceptions (cognitive processes) significantly influence our emotions and Behaviours. NLP techniques are designed to bring about changes in these cognitive processes to promote positive change.

Neuro-Linguistic Programming is a rich and complex field that offers valuable insights into human cognition and Behaviour. Its combination of practical techniques andunderstanding of cognitive processes makes it a powerful tool for personal development and therapeutic intervention. As we move forward in this book, we'll delve deeper into the integration of NLP with Cognitive Behavioural Therapy, showcasing how these two approaches can complement each other for improved therapeutic outcomes.

Cognitive Behavioural Therapy (CBT) is a therapeutic approach that has gained prominence due to its effectiveness in treating a wide range of psychological disorders. CBT is grounded in the belief that our thoughts, emotions, and Behaviours are intricately linked, and that changing our thought patterns can lead to significant changes in our feelings and Behaviours. To fully understand CBT, we need to look at its origins, foundational principles, theoretical underpinnings, and its effectiveness.

Evolution of Cognitive Behavioural Therapy

The roots of CBT can be traced back to the mid-20th century with the rise of two major therapeutic approaches: cognitive therapy, pioneered by Aaron T. Beck, and Behavioural therapy, which grew out of the work of B.F. Skinner and others. Cognitive therapy focused on the importance of cognitions or thoughts and how they affect our emotions and Behaviours. In contrast, Behavioural therapy emphasized observable Behaviours and how they are learned and maintained.

In the 1960s and 70s, these two approaches started to merge, creating a new therapeutic model known as Cognitive Behavioural Therapy. This approach recognized that both cognitions and Behaviours play a vital role in understanding and treating psychological disorders.

Fundamental Principles of Cognitive Behavioural Therapy

The core principles of CBT can be summarized as follows:

Incorrect or counterproductive methods of thinking can contribute to psychological issues.
In part, psychological issues stem from learned patterns of unhelpful behavior.
People with psychological issues can learn more effective coping mechanisms, thereby alleviating their symptoms and enhancing their effectiveness in life.

These principles form the basis for various techniques used in CBT, such as cognitive restructuring (changing unhelpful thought patterns), exposure (gradually and safely facing fears), and Behavioural activation (engaging in activities that are mood-enhancing).

Theoretical Underpinnings of CBT: Cognitive and Behavioural Theories

CBT is grounded in both cognitive and Behavioural theories. Cognitive theory posits that our thoughts or cognitions influence our emotions and Behaviours. If our thoughts are distorted or unhelpful, they can lead to negative emotions and maladaptive Behaviours. Therefore, by identifying and changing these unhelpful thought patterns, we can improve our emotional wellbeing and Behavioural responses.

Behavioural theory, on the other hand, focuses on the concept of conditioning or learning. It suggests that our Behaviours are learned responses to our environment and can be unlearned or relearned through techniques such as reinforcement, punishment, and modeling. Therefore, by changing our Behaviours, we can also change our thoughts and emotions.

Effectiveness of CBT in Treating Various Psychological Disorders

Over the past few decades, CBT has been extensively researched and has been found to be effective in treating a wide range of psychological disorders, including depression, anxiety disorders, post-traumatic stress disorder (PTSD), obsessive-compulsive disorder (OCD), eating disorders, and many more. Its effectiveness lies in its practical approach, focusing on the here and now, and providing individuals with skills that they can apply in their daily lives.

Cognitive Behavioural Therapy provides a versatile and effective approach to treating various psychological disorders. Its understanding of the intricate connections between thoughts, emotions, and Behaviours offers valuable insights into human cognition and Behaviour. As we continue to explore the integration of CBT with Neuro-Linguistic Programming, we will see how these two approaches can enrich each other for improved therapeutic outcomes.

Having established a comprehensive understanding of both Neuro-Linguistic Programming (NLP) and Cognitive Behavioural Therapy (CBT), this chapter will delve into the rationale and potential benefits of combining these two approaches. The shared elements and complementary aspects of NLP and CBT will be examined, underpinned by case studies and research findings.

Rationale for Combining NLP and CBT

NLP and CBT are complementary due to their shared emphasis on the mind and its influence on behavior. Both perspectives acknowledge that our thoughts, emotions, and behaviors are intrinsically interconnected. They both seek to effect positive change by identifying and altering detrimental thought patterns and behaviors.

NLP, with its rich set of techniques for understanding and influencing human experience, can offer additional tools for therapists practicing CBT. It can provide a different perspective and a new range of strategies to address cognitive and Behavioural issues. Thus, the integration of NLP techniques into

CBT may enhance therapeutic outcomes and offer a more personalized, client-centered approach.

Shared Elements between NLP and CBT

Several shared elements exist between NLP and CBT, including:

Focus on Thoughts, Emotions, and Behaviours: Both NLP and CBT recognize the crucial role of thoughts (cognitions) in shaping our emotions and Behaviours. They both aim to bring about positive change by working with these thoughts and the Behaviours they influence.

Goal-oriented Approach: Both NLP and CBT are goal-oriented, focusing on helping individuals achieve their desired outcomes. Both approaches work towards identifying and overcoming obstacles that prevent individuals from reaching these goals.

Here-and-now Focus: Both NLP and CBT emphasize the importance of the 'here and now.' While acknowledging the influence of past experiences, they focus on present thoughts and Behaviours and how these can be changed to improve future experiences.

Case Studies and Research Findings

Several case studies and research findings point towards the potential benefits of integrating NLP into CBT. For instance, research studies have indicated that certain NLP techniques, such as reframing and the use of metaphors, can enhance the effectiveness of CBT interventions for conditions like depression and anxiety.

Case studies also demonstrate the potential of this integration. For example, a client struggling with phobias might benefit from the combined use of CBT's exposure techniques and NLP's anchoring techniques to manage their fear response more effectively.

However, it's important to note that while promising, the research on the integration of NLP and CBT is still in its early stages. More rigorous studies are needed to substantiate these findings and provide a solid evidence base for this integrative approach.

The integration of NLP techniques into CBT presents an exciting avenue for enhancing therapeutic outcomes. While both approaches are powerful in their own right, their combination may offer a more comprehensive and flexible toolset to meet the diverse needs of individuals seeking psychological help. As we progress further into this book, we'll delve deeper into specific NLP techniques that can be integrated into CBT and explore the empirical evidence supporting this integrative approach.

In this chapter, we delve into the specifics of how Neuro-Linguistic Programming (NLP) techniques can enhance Cognitive Behavioural Therapy (CBT) practices. We focus on three primary techniques from NLP: reframing, anchoring, and the use of language patterns. Each of these techniques provides unique strategies for influencing thought processes and Behaviours, aligning perfectly with the objectives of CBT.

Reframing in NLP and CBT

Reframing is a core technique in NLP that involves changing the way one perceives an event or experience, thereby changing its meaning and impact. In the context of CBT, reframing can be an effective tool for challenging and changing maladaptive thought patterns.

For example, a client who consistently thinks, "I always fail; I'm a failure," can work with their therapist to reframe this thought to, "I didn't succeed this time, but that doesn't make me a failure. Each attempt brings me closer to success." This shift in perspective can help alleviate feelings of hopelessness and promote more adaptive Behaviours.

Anchoring and its Integration into CBT

Anchoring is another powerful NLP technique. It involves creating a 'trigger' or 'anchor' for a specific emotional state. This anchor can then be used to quickly access this emotional state when needed.

In a CBT context, anchoring can be used to help clients manage emotional responses more effectively. For instance, a client dealing with anxiety might establish an anchor for a calm and relaxed state. This anchor can then be used in situations that typically provoke anxiety, helping the client manage their response more effectively.

Language Patterns in NLP and their Role in CBT

Language patterns are a fundamental aspect of NLP, recognizing the power of language in shaping our thoughts, emotions, and Behaviours. Specific language patterns can be used to challenge and change unhelpful thought processes, aligning well with the objectives of CBT.

For example, a client might say, "I can't cope with this stress." A therapist could use language patterns to challenge this thought, saying, "You feel you can't cope with this stress right now. Can you think of a time when you felt similarly but were able to manage? What was different then?"

Practical Examples and Step-by-Step Instructions

To facilitate understanding and implementation, each of these techniques will be accompanied by practical examples and step-by-step instructions. These guides will provide a hands-on approach, enabling both therapists and clients to apply these techniques effectively within a CBT framework.

The integration of NLP techniques into CBT can provide additional strategies for challenging and changing unhelpful thought processes and Behaviours. The techniques of reframing, anchoring, and language patterns each offer unique strategies that align well with the principles of CBT, potentially enhancing therapeutic outcomes. As we progress further into this book, we'll continue to explore the integration of NLP and CBT, focusing on the empirical evidence supporting this approach and the ethical considerations involved.

In this chapter, we delve into the empirical evidence and research surrounding the integration of Neuro-Linguistic Programming (NLP) techniques in Cognitive Behavioural Therapy (CBT). A critical examination of these studies will provide insights into the effectiveness of this approach and its potential implications for clinical practice.

Review of Empirical Studies and Research

Several studies have examined the effectiveness of integrating NLP techniques into CBT. For example, research has explored the impact of reframing, an NLP technique, in enhancing the outcomes of CBT interventions for conditions such as depression and anxiety. Similarly, studies have also investigated the use of NLP anchoring techniques in managing emotional responses within a CBT framework.

These studies generally indicate that the integration of NLP techniques can enhance the effectiveness of CBT interventions. Clients who received CBT with integrated NLP techniques have often reported higher levels of satisfaction and better therapeutic outcomes compared to those who received standard CBT.

Evaluation of Research Methodologies: Strengths and Limitations

While these findings are promising, it's important to critically evaluate the methodologies of these studies. Many of the current studies are based on small sample sizes, which can limit the generalizability of the findings. Moreover, the majority of these studies rely on self-reported measures, which may be subject to bias.

On the other hand, the strengths of these studies lie in their innovative approach and the potential they showcase for enhancing therapeutic outcomes. They open up new avenues for research and underscore the need for further exploration into the integration of NLP and CBT.

Implications for Clinical Practice

The findings from these studies have significant implications for clinical practice. They suggest that therapists trained in CBT could potentially enhance their therapeutic outcomes by integrating specific NLP techniques into their practice. Furthermore, these findings also highlight the need for therapists to receive adequate training in NLP to ensure its effective and ethical application within a therapeutic context.

While preliminary research into the integration of NLP techniques into CBT is promising, more rigorous studies are needed to substantiate these findings. Nevertheless, these studies highlight the potential of this integrative approach and its possible implications for enhancing therapeutic outcomes in clinical practice. As we move forward, we'll explore the ethical considerations and challenges associated with this integration.

Chapter 6: Ethical Considerations and Challenges

The integration of Neuro-Linguistic Programming (NLP) techniques into Cognitive Behavioural Therapy (CBT) indeed presents promising therapeutic opportunities. However, it also brings forth certain ethical considerations and challenges. This chapter aims to explore these aspects, providing therapists with guidelines for ensuring the ethical and responsible application of NLP techniques within a CBT framework.

Ethical Considerations

Client Autonomy: NLP techniques are powerful tools for influencing thoughts and Behaviours. It's crucial that therapists respect clients' autonomy and ensure these techniques are used to facilitate clients' goals, not impose the therapist's agenda.

Informed Consent: Clients should be fully informed about the use of NLP techniques within their therapy sessions, including potential risks and benefits. They should have the opportunity to ask questions and decide whether they are comfortable with the integration of these techniques into their therapy.

Therapist Competence: Therapists integrating NLP techniques into CBT should be adequately trained in NLP. They should possess a deep understanding of these techniques and their application, ensuring they're used effectively and ethically.

Challenges and Limitations

While the integration of NLP and CBT holds promise, it also presents certain challenges and limitations:

Evidence Base: While preliminary research indicates potential benefits of integrating NLP into CBT, more rigorous studies are needed. The current evidence base is limited, and therapists should be cautious not to overstate the benefits of this integration.

Individual Differences: As with any therapeutic approach, the effectiveness of integrating NLP techniques into CBT will likely vary across individuals. Therapists should be attentive to individual differences and continually assess the suitability and effectiveness of these techniques for each client.

Time Constraints: Incorporating NLP techniques into CBT sessions might require additional time, which can be a challenge in settings where session lengths are fixed.

While the integration of NLP techniques into CBT offers promising possibilities, it's crucial to navigate this path with ethical considerations and potential challenges in mind. As we move forward, therapists should be encouraged to continue learning, practicing, and researching this integrative approach, always striving for the best possible outcomes for their clients.
Conclusion

In this book, we have embarked on a comprehensive exploration of the integration of Neuro-Linguistic Programming (NLP) techniques into Cognitive Behavioural Therapy (CBT). We started with a detailed examination of both NLP and CBT, understanding their origins, principles, and methodologies. This foundation allowed us to delve into the possibilities offered by their integration, examining the shared elements between the two and highlighting the potential benefits of this approach.

We discussed specific NLP techniques such as reframing, anchoring, and the use of language patterns, and explored how they could enhance the effectiveness of CBT interventions. Practical examples and step-by-step instructions were provided to facilitate understanding and implementation of these techniques within a therapeutic context.

Recognizing the importance of empirical evidence, we critically reviewed studies and research conducted on the integration of NLP techniques into CBT, acknowledging the strengths and limitations of existing research methodologies. While preliminary research suggests that this integration could enhance therapeutic outcomes, we stressed the need for more rigorous studies to substantiate these findings.

We also addressed potential ethical considerations and challenges associated with the integration of NLP into CBT, and provided guidelines for therapists to ensure ethical and responsible application of these techniques. It was emphasized that therapists should respect client autonomy, ensure informed consent, and strive for competence in their application of NLP techniques.

The journey through this book has illuminated the potential benefits and challenges of incorporating NLP techniques in clinical practice. The integration of NLP and CBT holds promise for offering therapists additional strategies for challenging and changing unhelpful thought processes and Behaviours, potentially enhancing therapeutic outcomes. However, it is also a journey fraught with challenges that require careful navigation.

As we conclude, it is evident that the exploration of NLP within the field of psychotherapy is far from over. We anticipate further research and practical applications to continue to enrich our understanding of this integrative approach. It is our hope that this exploration encourages therapists and researchers alike to continue to unlock the mind's potential and maximize the effectiveness of therapeutic interventions.

Rex Morton is a renowned author and researcher in the United Kingdom with a passionate interest in the human mind, specifically in Cognitive Behavioural Therapy (CBT) and Neuro-Linguistic Programming (NLP).

Morton has spent a considerable portion of his professional life diving deep into the theories and principles that form the backbone of these two compelling fields.

Although Morton does not have clinical experience, his intense curiosity and dedication to studying these subjects have made him a respected figure in the field. He has thoroughly researched the integration of NLP techniques into CBT, offering fresh perspectives and insights into how these two methodologies can complement each other to enhance understanding of human cognition and Behaviour.

As an author, Morton has successfully communicated his knowledge and passion to a broader audience, making complex psychological theories accessible to professionals and interested laypersons. His writing is characterized by a clear, engaging style and a focus on the practical application of theories, making them relevant to everyday life.

In his personal life, Morton is an ardent lover of the natural world, often spending his free time exploring the British countryside. His passion for landscape photography allows him to capture and share the beauty of these excursions. Despite his accomplishments, Morton is known for his humility and eagerness to continue learning. His work continues to inspire those interested in the intricate workings of the human mind and the exciting possibilities presented by the integration of NLP and CBT.

If you've found the content of this book enlightening and wish to continue your journey of understanding the human mind, I warmly invite you to visit my website at www.rexmorton.com. The website serves as a hub of knowledge where I share my latest findings, thoughts, and insights on NLP and related topics.

I also encourage you to subscribe to the newsletter available on the website. By subscribing, you'll receive regular updates on a range of topics, from detailed discussions on specific NLP techniques and their application in other fields to the latest research.

The newsletter is also the first place I'll share news of upcoming releases. Whether it's the announcement of a new book, the launch of an online course, newsletter subscribers will be the first to know. This is a great opportunity to continue learning directly from me, deepening your understanding of NLP and related topics, and enhancing your skills in applying these techniques in your own life or professional practice.
I'm looking forward to sharing this journey with you.

www.ingramcontent.com/pod-product-compliance
Lightning Source LLC
Chambersburg PA
CBHW060905260726
48661CB00008B/3470